This book belongs to:

____

Made in United States
North Haven, CT
20 November 2021

11321581R00067